ZION · BRYCE
NATIONAL PARKS

Text and Photos by
ANDREA PISTOLESI

© Copyright by Casa Editrice Bonechi - Firenze - Italia
Tel. +39 055 576841 - Fax +39 055 5000766
e-mail: bonechi@bonechi.it - Internet: www.bonechi.it

Printed in Italy by *Centro Stampa Editoriale Bonechi.*

ISBN 88-8029-021-5

* * *

INTRODUCTION

What do Zion and Bryce have in common? For one thing, they are both defined as "canyons". But while Zion is actually a canyon in the classic sense of the definition, a deep narrow gorge cut into the rock by a course of water, Bryce can best be described as a series of amphitheaters open to the sun and wind. Zion is the realm of shadows and twilight, of powerful rocky monoliths which dominate the scenery and leave little room for the sky. Bryce consists of vast panoramas that stretch out to an infinite horizon. As morning passes into noon and on to night, the changing nuances of color of the delicate sculptures of Bryce are one of the park's hallmarks.

Close to each other as they are, and both in Utah, a state settled by the Mormons, it is not surprising that their histories run parallel. Their early inhabitants were Indians. The Anasazi tribe lived in the Four Corners region until they disappeared from the scene in the thirteenth century for reasons that still remain obscure. The Spanish Dominguez-Escalante expedition encountered Indians from various Paiute tribes, but like other explorers (including Jedediah Smith in 1829) did not venture into the heart of Zion. Nor is there any record of anyone ever reaching Bryce. In any case, the arrival of the white man signalled the end of the Paiute civilization, already weakened by continuous hostilities with neighboring tribes. The arrival of the first Mormons from Salt Lake City in the mid-nineteenth century marked the beginning of what we can call more recent history in the area. These new settlers were more interested in cultivating available land, or turning it to pasture, than in the canyon's natural beauty. Although local landmarks were often discovered by non-Mormon explorers such as John Powell, it was the Mormons who gave them their names in accordance with their religious traditions and beliefs. An exception is Bryce, which was named for Ebenezer Bryce, one of the early settlers. Agriculture gradually became the leading activity and communities like St. George (capital of "Dixie Land") and Cedar City were founded. Further exploration heightened awareness of the importance of these canyons until they were finally declared National Parks (Zion in 1919, Bryce in 1923).

The appeal of this corner of the West lies in the works of nature, not of man. History here is seen in terms of geological eras, a long slow passage of time represented by a scientifically unique fissure in the earth's crust. Zion and Bryce are the highest part of a geological phenomenon that begins with the Grand Canyon. The so-called Grand Stairway is none other than an inclined orderly sequence of layers of rock. Each layer was created millions and millions of years ago and each type of rock that crops out is different. The rock strata of Grand Canyon are the oldest. They were virtually untouched by tectonic movement and offer a perfect cross section of the Paleozoic formation. The uppermost layer is called Kaibab limestone and forms the crust of the North and South Rims at the top of the Grand Canyon. Located close to the Moenkopi Formation at an altitude of 4000 feet above sea level, with respect to the Grand Canyon, the strata in this section of the Rockies are tilted northwards. This does not however interrupt or disturb the order of their formation. In Zion Canyon the series continues on a smaller scale with rock from the Triassic and Jurassic eras up to thick layers of Navajo sandstone. The steep walls of Zion belong for the most part to the vermilion-colored Chinle Formation. In the heart of the valley this is topped by a light-colored stone, also worn smooth by erosion. Above ground the same Navajo sandstone takes on a strikingly different appearance, as one can see in the White Cliffs along the Zion-Mt. Carmel Highway. There, the regularity of the valley gives way to a group of fanciful, pudding-shaped formations, the Hoodoos, which are part of the Checkerboard Mesa. These rocks are still relatively compact. At Bryce, the surface layers are composed of more recent and more fragile formations. The Pink Cliffs are an example of what can happen when time and weather wear away the rock, and the colors are more clearly evident. Similar types of rock, thanks to the effects of erosion, can produce a variety of spectacular scenery. Zion is a deep gorge carved into the rock by the Virgin River, fed by mineral-

GEOLOGIC SECTION	PERIOD	ERA

BRYCE CANYON

Wasatch — TERTIARY 1/70 million years ago — CENOZOIC

Kaiparowits

Wahweap — CRETACEOUS 70/130 million years ago

Straight Cliffs

Tropic Shale

Dakota

ZION CANYON

Carmel

Navajo — JURASSIC 130/160 million years ago — MESOZOIC

Kayenta

Moenave

Wingate

Chinle

Moenkopi

GRAND CANYON

TRIASSIC 160/200 million years ago

PALEOZOIC

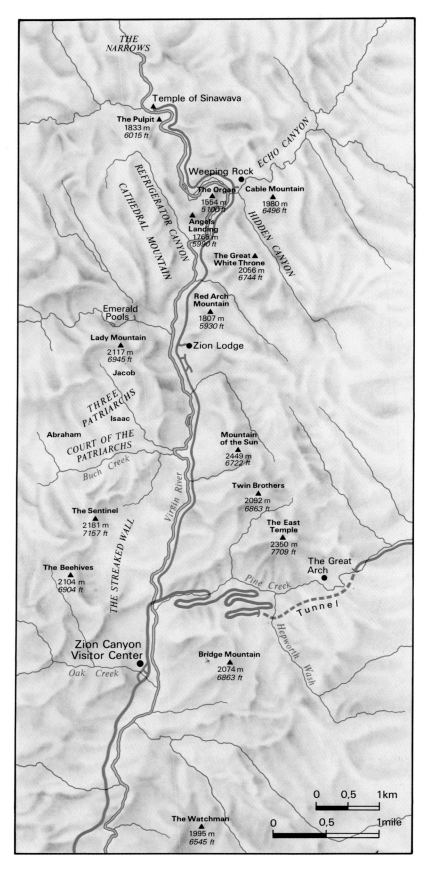

THE NARROWS

Temple of Sinawava ▲

The Pulpit ▲
1833 m
6015 ft

REFRIGERATOR CANYON

CATHEDRAL MOUNTAIN

ECHO CANYON

Weeping Rock ●

The Organ ▲
1554 m
5100 ft

Cable Mountain ▲
1980 m
6496 ft

HIDDEN CANYON

Angels Landing ▲
1765 m
5990 ft

The Great ▲
White Throne
2056 m
6744 ft

Red Arch
Mountain
▲
1807 m
5930 ft

Emerald
Pools

Lady Mountain
▲
2117 m
6945 ft

● Zion Lodge

Jacob

THREE PATRIARCHS

Isaac

Abraham

COURT OF THE
PATRIARCHS

Buch Creek

Mountain
of the Sun
▲
2449 m
6722 ft

Twin Brothers
▲
2092 m
6863 ft

Virgin River

The Sentinel ▲
2181 m
7157 ft

THE STREAKED WALL

The East
Temple
▲
2350 m
7709 ft

The Great
Arch ●

Pine Creek

The Beehives ▲
2104 m
6904 ft

Tunnel

Hepworth Wash

**Zion Canyon
Visitor Center** ●

Bridge Mountain
▲
2074 m
6863 ft

Oak Creek

0   0,5   1km

0   0,5   1mile

The Watchman
▲
1995 m
6545 ft

◄ *ZION CANYON*

rich tributary waters. As one
moves in along the Scenic Drive,
the surrounding mountains seem
to reach out and envelop the
visitor with the creation of what
are known as Hanging Valleys.
The soft Navajo sandstone
between one peak and the other
has been hollowed out by the
erosive action of the torrents
before they filter into the valley
below as waterfalls or seepage
and continue their work of
wearing down the stone. The
valleys rather than the peaks of
this false mountain range are
what characterize Zion. While at
Bryce it is light that transforms
the shapes and colors of the
landscape, at Zion it is water,
with its cascades and torrents,
and the rocky walls worn smooth
by the force of water.
The experience of travelling
through one canyon holds no
comparison with that of the other.
At Zion the major sights can be
seen from the Scenic Drive which
moves into the heart of the
canyon all the way to the outer
edge of the Narrows where the
smooth rock walls fall straight
down into the Virgin River. At
Bryce, the entire trail winds
around the edge of an imposing
amphitheater. Walking along a
natural terrace called the
Whiteman Bench, glimpses of
fantastic scenery appear among
the trees of Dixie National Forest.

BRYCE CANYON ►

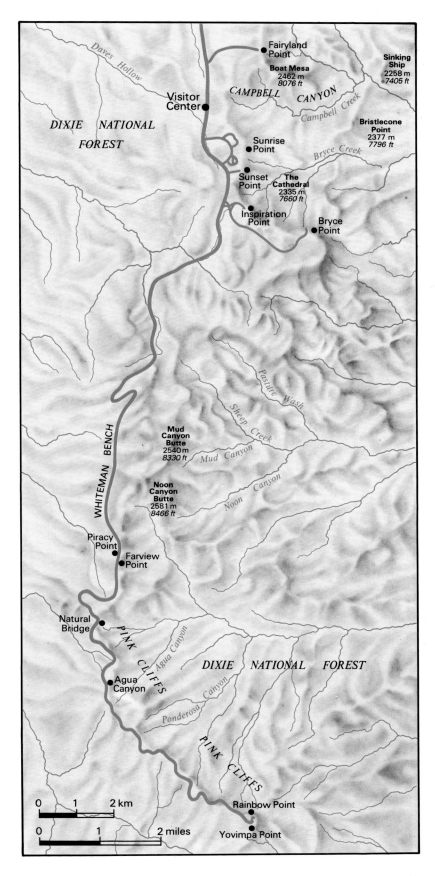

What strikes the visitor most are without doubt the famous Pink Cliffs. *Sculptured by erosion, their varied silhouettes are always impressive, whether grouped together in forests of stone as in the* Bryce Amphitheater, *or standing alone as in the* Natural Bridge *or* Agua Canyon. *The panorama of the cliffs between the green Pansaugent Plateau and Paria Valley is truly stunning. Bryce Canyon represents the highest step of the Grand Stairway. The various strata down to the depths of the Grand Canyon can be clearly identified by their differences in color as they crop out in the form of cliffs, natural sculptures, and monoliths which the Paiute Indians thought of as men condemned to immobility by the gods.*

In essence, the trip to Zion and Bryce is a sort of mixture of nature and mythology, scenery and history. The cliffs, the monoliths of vermilion-colored rock known as The Patriarchs, Angels Landing *and the* Temple of Sinawava, *the rose-colored monoliths with their poetic names,* Thor's Hammer, Sinking Ship *and* Sea Castle *fuse into a single whole in our memories. The geological aspect and the uniqueness of these sites which have stimulated man's fantasy both then and now are all part of our recollections of this visit.*

ZION CANYON

Coming in from the east, on the Zion-Mt. Carmel Highway, gives the visitor a chance to get a complete panorama of the particular environment of Zion. Upon descending to a level where the rock strata become visible, the abstract forms of the highest layer turn out to be exposed Navajo sandstone. The top consists of a variety of light-colored shapes, while the bottom is red and more compact. These candid profiles rightly deserve the name **White Cliffs**. Marine deposits dating back to a specific geological period, as in the other *Grand Stairway* strata, seem to be absent as indicated by the veins running through every visible surface. The formation here consists of solidified dunes, sandy deposits which slowly hardened into the irregular and whimsical **Hoodoos**. This porous and friable rock is easily worn away by rain and infiltrations of water and the result is a soft "gelatinous" landscape. A sparse vegetation of brush and fir trees survives in the small valleys where rainwater collects. Higher up, the smooth silhouette of the hills seems to fluctuate as their mass bears down on the land below. The largest and most interesting of these, 6670 ft. (20333 m.) high, is **Checkerboard Mesa**, so-called after the regular pattern that erosion traced on the walls. The road that leads into the park from Bryce Canyon and Grand Canyon passes right below the mesa and continues along the winding course of **Pine Creek**, which is usually dry except after violent thunderstorms. But the erosive force of this torrent is not to be taken lightly, as witnessed by the valley it has excavated on its way down to the Virgin River.

The Zion-Mt. Carmel Highway leaves the Navajo sandstone and moves to the edge of the canyon, passing through a long tunnel excavated in the bedrock. The **Tunnel** is a marvelous feat of engineering.

It is however the panorama of Zion glimpsed through two openings — a picture painted by the hand of nature and framed by an arch of stone — that lingers on in the memory.

The road winds down the southern side of the valley, carved out by *Pine Creek*, towards the bridge over the Virgin River. The view is impressive. On the other side, near the *Sentinel*, *Mount Spry* dominates the entrance to the canyon. The *Great Arch*, a natural blind arch created by a rock slide, rises up in the highest corner of the vermilion wall of stone. Few visitors come to Zion from the east; most arrive from the south, following the course of the Virgin River and pass through a gateway guarded by the *Watchman* to the east and *Mount Kinesava* to the west. The powerful embrace of these two giants is an excellent introduction to what lies ahead.

The *Zion Canyon Visitor Center* is the best place to plan a visit, collect informative material on the park and ask rangers about trail conditions. No visitor should ever attempt to explore the remote corners of the canyon on foot without taking these precautions.

Knowledge of meteorological conditions is essential before deciding to visit specific places.

Moreover the weather is generally so variable that any rash ventures are to be discouraged.

Two of Zion Canyon's principal landmarks are to be found outside the Visitor Center. One is the **Watchman** (facing page), its unmistakable profile dominating the right bank of the **Virgin River**. This monolith sculptured by time appears almost sinister at sunset. Although the Watchman is almost 6545 ft. (2000 m.) high, its power lies not in its altitude, but in the sensation it gives of pure light. Poetry aside, it is part of the first eastern massif bounded by the North Fork, which runs along the canyon, and the East Fork of the Virgin River.
The peaks on the opposite side of the valley are not at all like the Watchman. The **Towers of the Virgin** (above) rise up on an imposing wall like an enormous amphitheater. The highest peak, a powerful pure white monolith worn smooth by time, is 7505 ft. (2268 m.) high, and is known as the *Altar of Sacrifice*.
Its immaculate color run through with streaks of red and the high elevation all indicate that it is of Navajo sandstone. The *Towers of the Virgin* are the first peaks to be touched by the light of dawn, the most magical moment of the day as the rock is tinted by the rosy rays of early sunrise. As the light spreads, the striations on the cliff walls become more evident. They are the result of erosion by infiltrations of water, rich in mineral salts, not unique to this part of the canyon.

The real journey into the heart of Zion Canyon starts between *Mount Spry* and *The Sentinel*, right after the bridge over the Virgin River. The two rock cliffs seem to close in on the traveller as he enters. On the left the small *Birch Creek* lies at the base of one of the most magnificent sights in the park: the **Three Patriarchs** (pp. 14-15) which loom up over the **Court of the Patriarchs**. These three impressive formations, named after **Abraham** (facing page), Isaac and Jacob, are only partially visible from the valley, hidden behind the massive form of *Mount Moroni*. They are similar in proportion and height, as well as in the clearly visible geological sequence (characteristic of Zion Canyon) to be read on their rock faces. But the forms that time has given them are so different that the group seems to be comprised of three contrasting personalities. The imposing vertical rock face of *Abraham* in particular is topped by a dome of Navajo sandstone, in keeping with the

typical forms this material assumes, and contrasts sharply with the harshness of *Isaac*. On the other side of the valley, the cliffs rise up sheer over the river's course. The most striking peak, the **Mountain of the Sun** (above and following page), 6722 ft. (2449 m.) high, is of particular geological interest since it differs from the neighboring *Twin Brothers*. Both these peaks, and those of the *Three Patriarchs*, are divided by *Hanging Valleys*, river beds hollowed out in the form of lateral valleys by seasonal torrents as they rush along their course before tumbling down in waterfalls or being absorbed by surface sandstone. The cross sections of these valleys can be observed from below. Geologically the most interesting aspect is not the peaks along this rim but the intermittent zones. These "theoretical" processes have been subject to the action of erosion and time and the landscape today is rich in unusual and striking features.

Zion Lodge (above and preceding page) is situated at the center of the canyon where it briefly widens out. Here the valley is rich in vegetation and makes a perfect base for excursions on foot or horseback to the interesting places in the vicinity. A trail right in front of the lodge leads to the **Emerald Pools**. The first of these pools is formed by a small natural dam which closes the valley, and the water leaves in the form of a waterfall. The second pool, higher up, nestles at the foot of the imposing rock face on the north side of **Lady Mountain** and is unusually easy to reach. The pools were created gradually as the water stored in the sandstone above slowly filtered down into the terraces that had formed on the sides of the canyon, conferring an aura of intimate shadows on the sites in contrast with the vastness of the landscape below.

Moving on into the canyon behind Zion Lodge, the visitor enters one of the areas where a wealth of free-standing formations dominates the landscape. The Virgin River winds around the backbone of **The Organ** (above), a diaphragm of brown which resisted the river's erosive force and diverted its course. But the main feature that strikes the visitor at this point are the two colossi that dominate the narrowing of the canyon on either side. The unmistakable silhouette of **Angels Landing** (following page) rises up on the left bank, part of the same group as *The Organ*. It really does seem to be a perfect landing place for a divinity coming from above. This striking vermilion tower, 5990 ft. (1765 m.) high and about 400 meters above the course of the river, finds its counterpart in the even more impressive and unmistakable silhouette of **The Great White Throne** (p. 25), the colossus which once more obstructs the course of the river

after the bend just mentioned.
These two monoliths set across from each other mark the entrance to the narrowest part of Zion Canyon. The rock faces, so different in their morphology and color, loom over the road which now cannot choose but follow the course of the Virgin River. The few areas where trees can get a hold are limited to the pebbly banks along the river bed.
The erosion process set in motion by this apparently tranquil river is clearly visible in *Angels Landing*, whose shape is the result of the detachment of the higher blocks when fractures were created by the deterioration of the underlying strata. As the water incessantly ate into the rock, the slope, now covered with shrubbery, was formed, and sand and pebbles continue to be carried slowly downstream.
The Virgin belies its apparent tranquil aspect with the hidden destructive force of its waters.

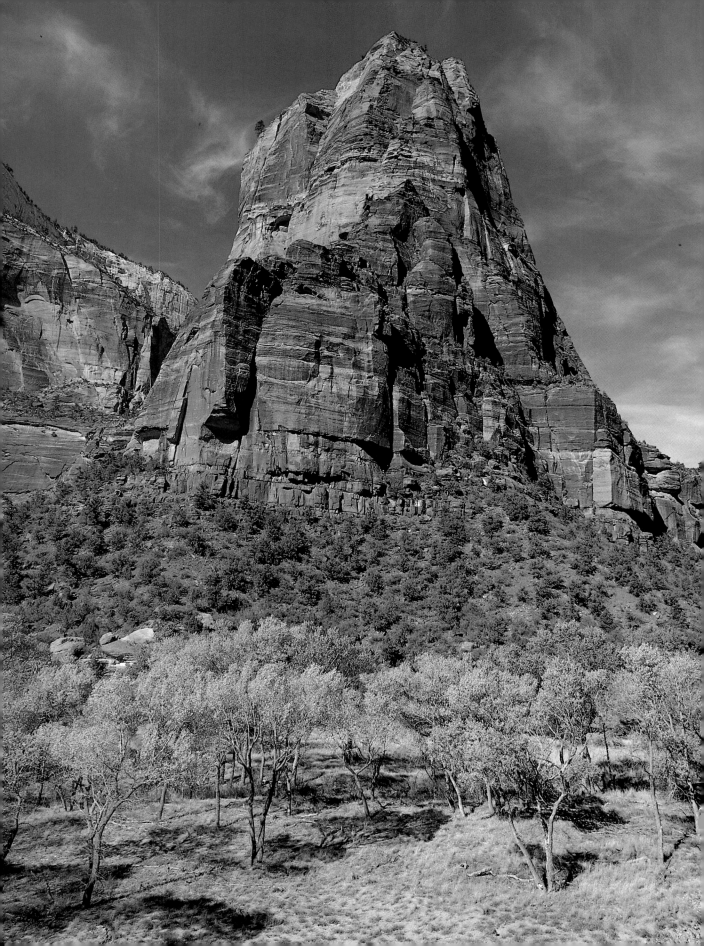

While the bottle-neck between *Angels Landing* and **The Great White Throne** (left) may seem to narrow down to a dead end, it is actually a base for excursions to hidden corners of the valley, as well as the starting point of a trail that leads back up to the rim of Zion Canyon.

The *Western Trail*, on the left bank of the Virgin River, climbs up across *Refrigerator Canyon*, a deviation leading to the summit of *Angels Landing*. Other trails branch off on the opposite slope, in the shadow of *Cable Mountain*. Explorations take one into *Hidden Canyon*, which lies behind the *White Throne*. Another trail, picturesque but long, climbs up through the shadows of *Echo Canyon*. *East Rim Trail*, which branches off here, is very difficult at points and ascends to an observation point more than 2200 ft. (600 m.) high overlooking the valley. No one should ever attempt to venture on these trails without previously consulting the rangers at the Visitor Center. Walking along the rims is dangerous when storms are brewing for lightning frequently strikes the mountain.

The full power of **The Great White Throne** makes itself felt on the return trip from the top of the canyon, when it suddenly looms into view behind the dark silhouette of *The Organ*, for in arriving from Zion Lodge the road passes right below. One of the most famous and impressive sights in Zion Canyon, this vast rock·face reflects the colors of the day. In the morning the shadows are softened by reflections from *Angels Landing* and from afternoon to evening it receives full sun, modifying the light-hued tones of its strata. The cap of Navajo sandstone (6744 ft. or 2056 m. above sea level, rising 2400 ft. or 700 m. above the canyon floor) and its full illumination by the sun, even though it stands in the heart of the canyon, give it the appearance of a hoary giant.

The inexhaustible water reserve in Zion Canyon is due to the extreme porosity of Navajo sandstone. With the exception of storms or melting snow, when the water rushes over the rims of the canyon and swells the torrents, normal rainfall usually filters into fissures in the thick surface strata and then eventually finds its way, somehow or other, to the Virgin River.

An example can be seen on the side opposite *The Organ*, at the beginning of *Echo Canyon Trail*. Two strata of different consistencies meet at the **Weeping Rock** and the water from above filters to the outside of the rock face where it forms an extensive dripping waterfall. The rock itself really does seem to ooze water. Phenomena of this sort, of smaller size, can be seen in other parts of Zion as well. The

multitude of flowers which form real hanging gardens in spring all depend on these sources of water.

Moving up into the heart of the canyon, the walls begin to close in. The Virgin River has cut its course almost vertically into the rock, which rises up behind a few trees which turn gold in autumn, contrasting with the vermilion tones of the gorge. The striae everywhere, caused by mineral salts, bear witness to the activity of water in this environment of stone which is not as uniform as it appears. The geometrical perfection of these forms reconfirms the variety of the constituent materials, not all subject to erosion to the same degree so that they fall in blocks rather than being gradually eaten away.

This is the last of the magnificent panoramas to be found within the rock walls of Zion Canyon. Before the Virgin River disappears, it runs through a gigantic amphitheater whose monoliths cancel the distinction between one side and the other. The site is so impressive that it has been given the name of **Temple of Sinawava** and it does indeed arouse a mystical feeling of religious awe. Man once built enormous monuments in honor of his God and to induce respect and fear in the faithful. Here the builder was nature herself.

The Scenic Drive which followed the course of the river ends here in the Temple of Sinawava and the walk across the narrows begins.

The *Temple of Sinawava*, like the *Great White Throne*, is the result of the erosion of a bend of

the Virgin River, except that it is relatively
more recent. So far water along the rim has
not yet hollowed out the hanging valleys or
lateral canyons which will eventually change
the monolithic nature of the surroundings. On
the other hand, the rock which, much like *The
Organ*, caused the river to deviate has eroded
much more rapidly. Nothing remains now but a
small rock which has been dubbed **The Pulpit**
thanks to its shape and position in the
"temple". Since the difference in level
between the *Temple of Sinawava* (4418 ft. or
1347 m. above sea level) and the *Zion Canyon
Visitor Center* (4000 ft. or 1219 m.) is relatively
small, the erosive energy of the Virgin River is
all the more impressive.

At **The Narrows**, the *Virgin River* becomes the main feature of the canyon. The rock faces, still imposing, smooth and vertical, draw ever closer to the point of almost closing out the sky. When the water level is low one can climb up inside these incredible surroundings, walking in the pebbly river bed itself. But before venturing off, it is essential to consult the rangers, for flash floods are possible at any time, as a result of the weather in distant places. The canyon remains faithful to its name: the rays of the sun never succeed in descending below the rims.

The Narrows mark the end of Zion Canyon, but the *National Park* continues for miles around in order to protect the *Hoodoos* in Navajo sandstone and other minor canyons. *Echo Canyon Trail* leads across this area up to the eastern entrance. On the opposite side, *West Rim Trail* climbs upwards to a vast plateau and arrives as far as *Lava Point*, the site of minor volcanic activity which involved Zion Canyon. The section of the park devoted to the *Kolob Canyons* can be reached from here, either on foot or along Highway 15. These canyons may not be as spectacular as the huge fissure hollowed out by the Virgin River, but they are still unusually interesting. A visit to the *Finger Canyons of Kolob*, so-called because of their number and arrangement, is recommended. Further on, at the end of a long trail, is *Kolob Arch*.

BRYCE CANYON

The geological differences between Bryce Canyon and Zion Canyon are evident even in the area leading up to the park entrance. The road climbs to the top of *Paunsaugunt Plateau*, with the pines and aspens of Dixie National Forest standing on either side. The Visitor Center is in a clearing; it is essential to stop there for information on the possible excursions and the condition of the trails. The road then follows the rim of the canyon, with various observation points overlooking the valley below. The first halting place is the most spectacular, with a view of the **Bryce Amphitheater** where the most characteristic scenery is concentrated. From **Sunrise Point** and **Sunset Point**, named for the beauty of the light at those times of day, the view fades away in the direction of the agricultural plain of Tropic. The world in between is brimming over with abstract shapes.

Bryce Creek hollowed out several small gorges in the rock and then rain and the infiltration of water, followed by frost, took care of the rest. It is the basic nature of the rock which goes to make up the *Wasatch*

Formation which is responsible for these abstract forms. A sedimentary material subdivided horizontally by a series of minor strata (bedding planes) which correspond to different eras and types of deposit, the varying consistency and compactness of these bedding planes offers a different degree of resistence to the elements. Vertically it is divided by fractures of tectonic origin (joints), produced by the general folding of the *Grand Stairway*. These weak points in a substance that was in itself already fragile, composed as it was of recently cemented small stones, were more prone to erosion and the result was scenery so rugged and hostile as to merit the name of **Badlands**.

This erosion process is particulary obvious from **Sunset Point** (pp. 40-41). A slope composed of eroded rock crops out from the rim of the plateau. The clusters of pinnacles which emerge consist of portions whose greater compactness makes them more resistant to the onslaught of time. But they too will eventually succumb in a never-ending cycle.

A formation which exemplifies the processes at work in this landscape stands right below *Sunset Point*. **Thor's Hammer** (another of those descriptive names inspired by the shape and size of this natural tower) owes its existence to the hardness of the uppermost stratum of rock. While it is not exactly a caprock, it served as such in that it warded off the ravages of weather, and as the ground around was washed downstream, the structure underneath remained isolated. Examples of similar erosion processes, although smaller, are numerous in the area, and this phenomenon is what created the sculptures of Bryce Canyon.

There are two other observation sites on the south side of the amphitheater in addition to Sunset Point: **Inspiration Point** and **Bryce Point** (above). The landscape here is much more rugged and the bottom of the canyon is filled with an intricate forest of rock pinnacles, evidence that the erosion process is less advanced. Or to put it another way, that it has gained a foothold on the plateau itself. The aspect of the land under *Inspiration Point* shows us what the area between Sunrise and Sunset Points looked like originally.

The rugged nature of the terrain and the lack of trails are such that the *Badlands* truly live up to the name. There are however three trails which start from Sunrise and Sunset Points: the circular *Fairyland*, and *Queen's Garden* and *Navajo Trail* which go towards the Valley of Tropic, making it possible to walk across this abstract world, which almost seems like a petrified forest. But under Inspiration Point it

becomes an impenetrable jungle.

Imaginative names abound. The dense group of spires next to Sunset Point, which look rather like skyscrapers, have been called the **Silent City** (facing page), for obvious reasons. A spur which offered more resistance to the hostile elements and which is only a bit lower than the plateau dominates the area. The top is known as **The Cathedral**, while the towers at the back are connected to each other but with fissures in between meriting the name of the **Wall of the Windows** (pp. 38-49).

A walk along the *Rim Trail* of the amphitheater is the best way to study the various aspects of this landscape, which the observer will enjoy interpreting in his own way, taking into account the effects of light that constantly vary the shapes of these rocks. Of all times of day the best are dawn and sunset, but an exploration of this "fairyland", whatever the moment, is always full of surprises.

The most magic moment in Bryce Canyon is, without a doubt, the **dawn**. The first light shows beyond the Paria Valley, brightening a sky that is almost always clear here in southern Utah, whatever the season, clouding over only when sudden storms appear, as short-lived as they are violent. As the sun climbs up over the horizon, an age-old ritual repeats itself. First the sunlight drives away the forest shades (on the top of the plateau), and then touches the first high towers of the amphitheater. The rays gradually move down to the lower groups, penetrate the gorges of the *Silent City*, hide behind *Thor's Hammer*, until they finally flood the entire valley announcing the beginning of a day which may be torrid in mid-summer or bitter cold in winter.

The best time to venture along the trails which slope down the canyon is in the early morning when the light falls on the surroundings but the sun is not yet at its zenith . When seen from close up with the rays of the sun penetrating their depth, the Badlands loom up as gigantic forms.

Navajo Trail, which starts right under *Sunset Point* and then passes near the slender precarious figure of **The Sentinel** (p. 52), is probably the most interesting trail in this morning light. The round trip is 2.2 miles (3.5 km.) long and takes about two hours of hard walking. The descent, which can be dangerous when the winter ice continues throughout the day, allows one to appraise the real dimensions of the formations from close up. They are much larger than they appear from the observation points. Not to speak of the diversity and consistency of the strata which are seen going backwards in time. The fractures were produced by water that penetrated and then expanded upon freezing, with the resulting strangely modulated transmogrification.

The point on the horizon where the "bright star of the morning" rises over the horizon changes from one day to the next with the passing of the seasons. And as the sun's rays strike the rocks from a different angle, their shapes seem to change.

The same sculptured rock formation may have a drastically different aspect in winter than in summer. An important role in these changing effects is also played by the snow, brought by the storms which streak across the Rockies, and which may linger on for months in the gorges of Bryce Canyon and reflect the light. **Winter dawn** is the most magic time of all; the soft mantle clothing the slopes now muffles the dense shadows of the fir trees which in summer lie dark on the canyon floor. For those who are unfamiliar with the site, it is hard to believe that with the coming of summer this blanket of snow will disappear for it seems

such an integral part of the landscape.

After the first snows, the trails freeze over completely and are too steep to be followed to the more secluded places. The park, however, remains open all year round, as does the road along the rim, except for the first few hours after a snowfall. The **Rim Trail** around the amphitheater is also accessible though ice remains a hazard.

Behind the canyon, even the *Paunsaugunt Plateau* changes its appearance with the changing of the seasons. In winter the thick verdant forest which guarantees shade throughout the day from spring on, looks like a vast ivory carving. Trees and clearings are covered with frozen snow and the reverberations of light are blinding. Animals which live here hibernate throughout the winter.

The road proceeds along the rim of the plateau, the so-called *Whiteman Bench*, a route that runs through the forest, opening out from time to time on the panorama of the *Pink Cliffs*. The same itinerary along the canyon can also be undertaken at the bottom, along the *Under-the-Rim Trail*, a relatively easy hike, intersected by connecting trails that lead to the road overhead. Whether seen from one side or the other, this is the most complete view of the sculptures that time has created in the gallery of Bryce Canyon.

The first halting place after *Farview Point* is **Natural Bridge**, a formation unequalled in the park in shape and size and which frames a panorama of *Bridge Canyon*. The origins of such a shape are characteristic of the area. While the surface stratum, now the upper part of the arch, remained compact, erosion ate its way into those below with greater efficacy. Infiltrated water froze and swelled in the vertical joints and eventually blocks of rock fell off, forming the huge opening in the wall of stone. Successive weathering rounded off the

corners. The slope surrounding the bridge is an exemplary demonstration of why vegetation is so sparse under the rim. The detritus which makes up the terrain is so friable and subject to landslides that few plants succeed in taking root. The entire Wasatch Formation is characterized by these sediments which are the remains of lacustrine deposits that were raised more than 13 million years ago, relatively recently geologically speaking, and are rich in non-cemented or incoherent fragments, plant and animal fossils, varying greatly in the methods of deposit and the periods. It is just this which makes them so fragile and at the same time perfect material for sculptures in continual evolution.
Agua Canyon is the next observation point on the 35-mile-long road. The panorama here spreads out over the **Paria Valley**, characterized by the green of the Dixie National Forest. A pinnacle of notable dimensions rises up from the jagged sides of the canyon, the size once more a consequence of the resistance offered by the uppermost stratum. The formation of the landscape depends in great part on the differences in composition of the various strata, clearly to be seen in this steep section. While the striking shapes of the sculptures are likely to catch the eye, note should also be taken of the effects of the stratigraphic division. The rock faces under the rim have been washed away and their sediment is proportional to the compactness of the stratum to which they

belong. The different colors of these strata explain the apparently random mosaic of Agua Canyon.

At its end, the rim on the Pink Cliffs of Bryce and the road along it, separate into two lookouts called **Rainbow Point** and **Yovimpa Point** (following pages). Looking northwards (p. 62), the vertical rock face of the light-hued canyon stretches out for miles to the horizon. It is from here that the best overall view of these cliffs is to be had. For the first time in Bryce Canyon, it is pure size, rather than the richness of the rock formations, that amazes us, although the power of these arabesqued mosaics in this vast landscape never fails to leave a deep-lasting impression.